RAILWAY
PRESERVATION
IN BRITAIN

Bob Gwynne

SHIRE PUBLICATIONS

Published in Great Britain in 2011 by Shire Publications Ltd, Midland House, West Way, Botley, Oxford OX2 0PH, United Kingdom.

44-02 23rd Street, Suite 219, Long Island City, NY 11101, USA.

E-mail: shire@shirebooks.co.uk   www.shirebooks.co.uk

© 2011 NMSI Trading Ltd.

Every attempt has been made by the Publishers to secure the appropriate permissions for materials reproduced in this book. If there has been any oversight we will be happy to rectify the situation and a written submission should be made to the Publishers.

A CIP catalogue record for this book is available from the British Library.

Shire Library no. 638.   ISBN-13: 978 0 74781 041 4

Bob Gwynne has asserted his right under the Copyright, Designs and Patents Act, 1988, to be identified as the author of this book.

Designed by Tony Truscott Designs, Sussex, UK and typeset in Perpetua and Gill Sans. Printed in China through Worldprint Ltd.

11 12 13 14 15   10 9 8 7 6 5 4 3 2 1

COVER IMAGE

The Bluebell Railway's Branch Line Weekend in 2009. *Fenchurch* hauls restored carriages and assorted wagons.

TITLE PAGE IMAGE

The *Duke of Gloucester* hauls a train on The Cauldon Lowe branch line in Staffordshire.

CONTENTS PAGE IMAGE

In the 1970s, The Great Western Society at Didcot looked to run mainline excursions and gradually built up their own vintage train. Here 7808 *Cookham Manor* and 5900 *Hinderton Hall* are seen hauling the train in October 1979, a few months before it was forced off the main line by new rules that barred wooden-bodied rolling stock.

ACKNOWLEDGEMENTS

Author's collection, 13 (bottom), 28 (top); Author, 10 (bottom), 13 (top), 39, 40, 45 (top), 49 (top), 50, 51, 59 (top), 60 (bottom); Steve Banks, 3; Reg Batten, 15; Eddie Bobrowski, 58; Tom Burnham, 38 (bottom); Ken Chown / Bluebell Railway Archive, 28 (bottom); Bluebell Railway Archive, 30 (top); David Christie, 26; Geoff Cryer, 29 (bottom), 33, 47; Dr Peter Darke, 60 (top); Festiniog Railway Archives, 45 (bottom); M. R. Gilkes / Middleton Railway Trust Archive, 4; Doug Hewson, 23 (top); Brian Hicks, 30 (bottom); John Harvey, Gresley Society Archive, 20 (bottom); Highland Railway Society, 24; David Gibson, title page; Adrian Knowles / GWS, 55 (bottom); KWVR Archive, 31; Bob Meanley, 54; Middleton railway Trust Archive, 20 (top); Ray O'Hara, 56; Robin Patrick, 34, 52, 59 (bottom), 61 (top); Paul Pettitt, cover image; Geoff Plumb, 25 (bottom); John R. Hume / RCAHMS, 35; Talyllyn Railway Archive, 18 (top and bottom); Cliff Thomas, 29 (top), 57 (top); Andrew P. M. Wright, 61 (bottom); William Wright, 36. All other images NRM / Science and Society. The Author would like to thank all those whose help and advice made this book possible.

THE NATIONAL RAILWAY MUSEUM

The National Railway Museum (NRM), York is the largest railway museum in the world. Its permanent displays and collections illustrate over 300 years of British railway history, from the Industrial Revolution to the present day. The NRM archive also includes a fabulous collection of railway advertising posters charting the history of rail. Visit www.nrm.org.uk to find out more.

This book is produced under licence from National Museum of Science and Industry Trading Limited. Royalties from the sale of this book help fund the National Railway Museum's exhibitions and programmes. The National Railway Museum Collection is a registered trademark, no. 2309517.

Unless otherwise credited, all images are courtesy of National Railway Museum / Science and Society Picture Library.

Shire Publications is supporting the Woodland Trust, the UK's leading woodland conservation charity, by funding the dedication of trees.

CONTENTS

INTRODUCTION: ENTHUSIAST NATION

Members of the Middleton Railway Preservation Society and visitors pose in front of the society's newly acquired brake van in January 1961. By then railway preservation was gaining notice in Britain and abroad.

Bᴿɪᴛᴀɪɴ at the start of the 1950s was a very different place from that of today. Sugar and petrol were still rationed, there were no motorways, most people worked on Saturdays and 'national service' meant you could still be conscripted to fight a war of the Government's choosing. If illness and unemployment no longer presaged disaster in the wake of the creation of the Welfare State, for many, indoor bathrooms, central heating and electrical gadgets galore (including television) were still the unlikely world of the Festival of Britain, a great show but not real life. Real life was lived in smoggy towns to a background chatter of a Cold War with an old ally, and the possible threat of nuclear annihilation. Real life was also a love affair with all things American,

best seen through music and film but also stretching to the planned rebuilding of historic towns like Coventry with more than a hint of Los Angeles.

Threaded through this world was steam: from factory hooters to night expresses, Britain was still living in the steam age. Steam-hauled trains, providing rhythmic continuity with the perceived certainties of the Victorian age, still ran to nearly everywhere in Britain and still seemed worthwhile. Indeed, a renewal programme had just started to build new 'standard' locomotives to help replace worn-out Victorian machines, and private factories still churned out steam locomotives for export to the colonies and elsewhere.

It was at this time, in an obscure part of rural mid-Wales, that a group of individuals came together to run an exhausted Victorian narrow-gauge railway. All clearly eccentric (or so the press thought at the time), the members of the Talyllyn Railway Preservation Society were led by a self-styled Edwardian gentleman writer, their quaint endeavours later subtly celebrated in the hit film, *The Titfield Thunderbolt*. 'Their' railway (and not the state's – some still objected to the recent nationalisation) ran from a resort that had never quite taken off, not quite to a village built to service an industry recently closed.

It was an unlikely start to the world of volunteer-operated 'heritage railways', which are now major earners in the UK tourism industry. It was also an unlikely harbinger of a Britain where history is now often celebrated by individuals working together, their projects rarely seeking or gaining official sanction at the outset.

This book is a brief introduction to the history of railway preservation and celebrates Britain's heritage railways – their ancestry, birth and development, and their future as an integral part of a nation comfortable with its past as the first industrial nation.

The appeal of the steam railway is clear from this K&WVR poster from the 1980s. Today most steam railways operate 'driver experience courses', earning useful additional income from those with the money, but not the time, to 'go through the grades' (in the time-honoured steam age way) and become locomotive drivers at the steam railway of their choice.

THE PAST ON A PEDESTAL

IN 1851, with the British economy roaring along to world domination, Prince Albert, the German husband of Queen Victoria, decided to celebrate the best of Britain's industrial might. The Great Exhibition was the first truly national mass event, with the growing train network able to deliver millions of people to view its marvels. It set some to thinking about the origins of this transport phenomenon. *Rocket*, the premium engine that had started this revolution, was pulled off a scrap siding in Cumbria and made ready for display at the exhibition.

Rocket never made it to London but it was at least 'preserved' and ready for the call, when it came, to become a part of the Patent Office Museum, the precursor to London's Science Museum. The museum opened in June 1857 as a direct result of the Great Exhibition. In the North East, perhaps prompted by this, Stephenson's *Locomotion* of 1825 (used as a humble pumping engine since 1841) was taken out of service and proudly displayed on a plinth at Darlington. Railway preservation, which had started by accident when the Canterbury and Whitstable Railway's *Invicta* had been left in a shed in 1839, had now officially begun.

Bennet Woodcroft, a noted inventor and former Professor of Descriptive Machinery at University College London, was the founder of the Patent Office Museum. He worked with the industrious first curator of the museum, F. P. Smith, to acquire more significant exhibits including in 1862 *Puffing Billy*, the world's oldest surviving locomotive (built in 1813). *Puffing Billy* was initially on loan until a purchase price could be agreed, as its owner deemed it to be 'still useful'.

Woodcroft and Smith clearly hit a chord with their work, even though at that time Britain's railways were still expanding. The remains of Timothy Hackworth's *Sans Pareil*, once *Rocket*'s rival at the Rainhill locomotive trials in 1830, were offered to the museum by businessman John Hick who agreed to pay the cost of 'putting it into something like presentable appearance'. The remains were being used as a pumping engine at Coppull Colliery, Lancashire, and true to his word Hick gathered what he could find and

Opposite:
The Rail Transport Gallery at the Science Museum in London in 1925. *Puffing Billy* leads a line of early locomotives flanked by display cases.

Puffing Billy's sister locomotive *Wylam Dilly* photographed with William and George Hedley (in top hats). In 1836 their father, William Hedley, publicly disputed that Stephenson was 'the father of the locomotive'; this helped ensure both of these historic machines were preserved. In 1882 *Wylam Dilly* was acquired by the Edinburgh Museum of Science and Arts.

courtesy of the London and North Western Railway, *Sans Pareil* was transported to London in 1864 looking something like it had in 1829. Francis Webb, later LNWR Chief Mechanical Engineer, and already Crewe Works Manager, may well have had an influence over its free passage. Webb allowed some ancient machines to be preserved at Crewe and in 1882 rescued an

Invicta hauling the opening train of the Canterbury and Whitstable Railway. The line opened four months before the Liverpool and Manchester Railway in 1830 and was mostly rope hauled. *Invicta* was built immediately after *Rocket* but was 'retired' by 1836 and put in store.

Columbine, built for the Grand Junction Railway at Crewe in 1845, pictured at the National Railway Museum in 1981. The locomotive was threatened with scrapping in the 1930s at a time when other ancient locomotives stored by the LMS were cut up.

early Trevithick boiler (possibly the remains of the very first passenger engine *Catch Me Who Can*) from a Hereford scrap heap.

This was the world of preservation by powerful men able to act at will, not a consistent approach to preserving Britain's heritage; in 1906 several broad-gauge locomotives were cut up at Swindon having been stored there since before the end of the broad gauge in 1892. *Lord of the Isles* of 1851 had actually been used as a promotional tool (in Edinburgh in 1890, Chicago in 1893 and London in 1897) but it was still scrapped. The Swindon axe had been wielded courtesy of George Churchward. William Stanier, then a rising star at Swindon, would later go on to do the same thing with locomotives preserved at Derby when he took over as Chief Mechanical Engineer on the LMS in 1932, despite the LMS supposedly having a pro-museum policy. (They had just used *Lion* – a Liverpool and Manchester locomotive of 1841, rescued by the Liverpool Engineering Society in 1927 – in their centenary celebrations.) An attempt to cull the Crewe collection (including the locomotive *Columbine*, then erroneously believed to have been the first locomotive to have been built there in 1845), was surprisingly and robustly headed off by the workers. Clearly there was nascent sentiment for railway artefacts of the past amongst the 'lower orders' even in the hard world of the inter-war period.

Public relations generally worked in preservation's favour, especially if the ancient machines showed how much the locomotive had progressed, or (as with *Locomotion*) they engendered company pride. The North Eastern Railway had capitalised on this in 1875 with their major celebration of the fiftieth anniversary of the opening of the Stockton and Darlington railway, an event

George Stephenson's *Locomotion*, which opened the Stockton and Darlington railway in 1825, on display at Darlington's main station. This was the locomotive's main 'home' between 1892 and 1975.

Liverpool and Manchester 'Luggage Engine' *Lion* of 1838 en-route to 'Steamport' railway museum in Southport in 1980. Star of the Ealing comedy *The Titfield Thunderbolt*, *Lion* is now on display at the Museum of Liverpool. 'Steamport' closed to the public in 1997, the stock forming the basis of the Ribble Steam Railway (opened 2005).

that cost them more than £5,000 (equivalent to nearly £500,000 today). The show featured some twenty-seven locomotives, from the very latest to *Locomotion*, which was made to appear as though it was in steam. It led to the preservation of yet more 'relics', proving that the history of the railway industry had public appeal. The event was repeated in 1925, prompting the Great Western Railway to build a replica of the broad gauge locomotive *North Star*. Parts of the original engine that had been squirrelled away at Swindon works were used, including the driving wheels. The 1925 event also led to the establishment of a Railway Museum at York which attracted 18,000 people on its opening day in 1928. The initial display was largely the result of the collecting zeal of two of the North Eastern Railway's senior employees, H.J. Rudguard and J.B. Harper, who had gathered historic material at their offices in York during the course of their work across the North East.

Company pride had earlier seen the Furness Railway place its oldest surviving locomotive – nicknamed 'Old Coppernob' – in its own miniature 'Crystal Palace' at Barrow-in-Furness station in 1898; the narrow-gauge Padarn Railway also had its own private museum by 1886.

With the Science Museum gaining a de facto railway museum area, some leading enthusiasts, including the journalist Charles Rous-Marten, agitated for the establishment of a National Railway Museum. (Norway had led the way with this when they opened just such a museum in 1896.) Rous-Marten's timing of the GWR's *City of Truro* on the Ocean Mails in 1904 at 100 mph would ensure the preservation of the engine at York in 1931. His excited reports of the 'Races to the North' in 1895 influenced the preservation of the great rivals in that series of publicity stunts: GNR No. 1, the elegant 'Stirling Single', and LNWR *Hardwicke*.

The growing all-round interest in railways had by 1897 led to the establishment of *Railway Magazine*, aimed squarely at 'railwayacs' (railway enthusiasts), whether they were working in the railway industry or not. Clubs for enthusiasts had also started, including the Railway Club (1899) and the Stephenson Locomotive Society (SLS) in 1909. By then the idea of locomotive preservation was clearly established. An early rescue was the preservation of *Agenoria* in 1884

The original *North Star* of 1837 was scrapped in 1906. This replica was built at Swindon to star in the 100th anniversary celebration of the opening of the Stockton and Darlington Railway in 1925. The replica used parts of the original (including the wheels) which had been 'stored' at the works.

Furness Railway's 'Old Coppernob' on display outside Barrow-in-Furness station in the 1930s. Having hauled its first passenger train in 1846 the locomotive was preserved in 1898 in this mini 'Crystal Palace'. The building was destroyed by bombing in the Second World War; the locomotive's iconic copper firebox cover still bears the scars.

The recently
restored *Agenoria*
at Shutt End
Ironworks,
Staffordshire
in 1884.
E. B. Marten, one
of the first known
'preservation'
activists, may be
the man seated
in the centre of
the picture.

(originally built in 1829 by Rastrick, a judge at the Rainhill trials), the result of action by boiler inspector and engineer E.B. Marten. Marten persuaded the owner to restore it to 'museum' condition with an initial display in nearby Wolverhampton followed by a move to join *Rocket* in London. Other railway artefacts were also surviving in a kind of scattered railway Valhalla. In 1888 some original Bodmin and Wadebridge railway vehicles of 1834 were

City of Truro arrives
at York Railway
Museum in 1931
at the start of
its career as
a preserved
locomotive: 18,000
people visited the
Museum on its
opening day
in 1928.

plinthed at Waterloo by the London & South Western Railway. *Locomotion* had already been preserved with some 'Chaldron' coal wagons – the latter the start of a more humble strand of railway preservation that would lead eventually to the phenomenon of 'demonstration freight trains'.

In 1926 Dr H.A. Whitcombe of Weybridge managed to get a steam tram preserved (a locomotive under its skirts) and transported from Portstewart in Northern Ireland to Hull, where it joined a regional museum with a growing transport-related collection. The following year the SLS were instrumental in persuading the new Southern Railway management to preserve the LB&SCR locomotive *Gladstone*, the first group of enthusiasts to do so. They were led by John Nevil Maskelyne, who had long been involved with miniature railways. Maskelyne was on the inside of a quiet revolution that gave a rich few, and their close friends and servants, practical experience of running a real railway outside the vast railway industry.

One of leaders of this different approach to railways was 'gentlemen engineer' Sir Arthur Heywood, who developed what he saw as the minimum gauge for practical use (15-inch gauge), and demonstrated it in the greatest

Portstewart Tramway No. 1 was preserved by Dr Whitcombe in the Hull Museum of Commerce and Transport, the first museum of its kind, opened in 1925. The museum was destroyed in the Second World War, but No. 1 survived and is now in the Streetlife Museum in Hull.

Ella on the Duffield Bank Railway, which ran from 1874 to 1916 and was built to demonstrate 15-inch gauge as the minimum practical gauge for railways. By 1905 Blackpool had its own 'pleasure' railway. Parts of *Ella* are incorporated in the Ravenglass and Eskdale Railway's diesel *Shelagh of Eskdale*.

Gladstone on display at Waterloo just after preservation in 1926; behind it is the brand new Lord Nelson, 'Britain's most powerful passenger engine'. The fee to visit both cabs was 3d.

The poster advertising the newly preserved Gladstone. Few would have predicted that Lord Nelson would itself be preserved at the end of its working life in 1962, and subsequently be restored to working order.

See the last of
an old Friend!

"GLADSTONE" (1882)
is to be preserved in
S. Kensington Museum.

To-day she is in

No. 12 Platform

with the
"LORD NELSON" (1926)
Britain's most powerful passenger engine.

Inspect them both!
Admission 3d.
(devoted to Railway Orphanage. Woking.)

ever garden railway at his home near Derby from 1881. It was perhaps inevitable that people would want to capture the magic of trains via miniature lines that they could control themselves and Heywood showed one way this was possible. His approach was cheap to build and run but could do real work, and transport people considerable distances. He used techniques familiar to a growing number of model engineers, who had their own magazine, *Model Engineer*, from 1898.

The hobby would have a lasting practical influence on preserved railways.

The Ravenglass and Eskdale Railway re-opened in 1916, having been converted to 15-inch gauge by Northampton businessman and engineer Wenman Joseph Bassett-Lowke, working with Henry Greenly, the first engineer to design practical small-scale locomotives with a 'mainline' outline (comprising a long boiler and separate tender).

Bassett-Lowke, whose business had started by supplying components to model engineers, had gone down the leisure railway route after noting the favourable reaction that a 15-inch gauge railway had received at the Glasgow International Exhibition in 1901. This had used equipment by the Cagney brothers of America. Bassett-Lowke established 'Miniature Railways of Great Britain' in 1904, the start of a new phenomenon in Britain – the railway that exists purely as a leisure ride. The first successful line ran in Blackpool in 1905. A number of Greenly and Bassett-Lowke's clients were rich gentlemen looking to experience the pleasures of their own steam railway.

After the First World War, two such men, both racing-car drivers, decided to collaborate to build their own one-third scale main line because they believed the steam-hauled express would soon be a thing of the past. Captain Howey was a former pilot who had survived being shot down over the Western Front, and Count Louis Zbrowski owned a series of famous racing cars, each called 'Chitty Bang Bang'. Zbrowski was killed whilst driving for Mercedes at Monza in 1924 after the project had started. The railway realised by Henry Greenly was a complete double-track main line in miniature – the Romney, Hythe and Dymchurch Railway. The line quickly became famous, even acquiring its own armoured train in the Second World War. John Snell, one of the Talyllyn's first volunteers, would eventually become its manager after the Howey era had run its course.

By the end of the Second World War, Britain had a long (if erratic) tradition of preserving historic locomotives and other rolling stock, and of amateurs lobbying for this to be done. The idea that railways could exist purely for 'leisure' was also well established. The stage was set for a writer and visionary interested in preserving the functionality of machines for future generations, to take on a seemingly lost cause and create something new – the 'heritage railway'.

The first rail tour for enthusiasts: 'The Old Flying Scotsman' ran in from Kings Cross to Peterborough in September 1938. Seven six-wheeled carriages were hauled by the 'Stirling Single' (preserved in 1916). It was restored to working order in 1938 in a publicity move to highlight progress on the East Coast Main Line.

DOLGOCH STATION
ON THE
TALYLLYN RAILWAY
TOWYN MERIONETH WALES

ROLT'S REVOLUTIONARIES

IN 1949 *Picture Post* (a documentary magazine with a readership equivalent to those who watch the more 'serious' TV channels today) published an article about a railway. No ordinary railway, but one that the cartoonist Roland Emett was particularly keen on, as it appeared to be the living embodiment of his Far Twittering and Oysterperch Railway, a cartoon creation that had charmed the nation via the pages of *Punch*. This was the Talyllyn Railway in mid-Wales, at that stage staggering on into the post-war world completely unmodernised from Victorian times, and subsidised out of the back pocket of the local MP, Sir Haydn Jones.

When Jones died in 1950 a number of people got to thinking about whether the line could be saved. These included Owen Prosser, who went on to be the founding father of a rail lobby group that was to fight subsequent cuts in the network; and a writer with a recent bestseller (*Narrow Boat*) whose reputation was then just growing, Tom Rolt. Rolt wrote to his local paper and from the meeting that followed a committee was formed to keep the line running. A mild flirtation with the idea of conversion to 15-inch gauge led to links with local leisure railway owner and Midlands businessman John Wilkins, and to the TR's first fitter/engineer David Curwen.

Rolt's fame as an author, and his contacts with all quarters of London society, led to support from all directions. John Betjeman sent a donation and the new society later had Lord Northesk, cousin to the Queen Mother, as its President. Wilkins meanwhile supplied materials, money and access to insurance to get things started; at a time of timber rationing he even had access to railway sleepers via a licence for the nearby 15-inch gauge Fairbourne Railway (which he owned) granted on the basis that it was a transport link! He also had contacts among the engineering and business community of Birmingham, which had long seen this part of the North Wales coast as one of its main recreational areas. With Maskelyne of the SLS and saviour of *Gladstone* as Vice-President, the little railway very much had friends everywhere.

Opposite:
A poster from 1960 of Dolgoch Station on the Talyllyn Railway by Terence Cuneo for British Railways. By this time the Talyllyn was well established and proving that volunteer-supported steam railways could be effective tourist attractions.

The Talyllyn Railway Preservation Society's first train at Rhydyronen, pictured on 14 May 1951. The young fireman in the cab of the locomotive is John Snell who later became Manager of the Romney, Hythe and Dymchurch Railway.

An early working party on the Talyllyn Railway in 1951 with (left) John Wilkins, then Managing Director of Servis, manufacturer of washing machines and other domestic appliances at a time when sales of these items were booming.

The first few years were immortalised in Rolt's bestselling book *Railway Adventure* and in the film *The Titfield Thunderbolt* written by T. B. Clarke. He had holidayed in Towyn (now Tywyn) in 1952 and had seen a notice that read, 'volunteer platelayers wanted'. These years established the idea that volunteers could work on something not connected with religion or some conventional charitable purpose. They could also 'win one back' from the crushing conformity (as Rolt and others saw it) of the newly nationalised railways. They could even stand up for rail against the spirit of the age – modernisation and the motor car. The struggles of the Talyllyn Railway Preservation Society in the early 1950s would inspire a generation. It quickly spawned the revival of the Festiniog railway, thanks in part to a chance meeting between Lord Northesk of the Talyllyn and businessman enthusiast, Alan Pegler.

By 1955 change was very definitely in the air: British Railways' modernisation plan had announced the impending death of steam and the need to close some duplicate routes. Within five years there would be a standard-gauge railway preservation scheme, the Bluebell Railway (formed out of opposition to a pre-Beeching closure) and two contrasting narrow-gauge schemes, the Welshpool and Llanfair (a rural

branch line) and a 'leisure' line, the Lincolnshire Coast Light Railway, which was built with rails once used to transport Lincolnshire potatoes. There would also be an industrial line, based on an ancient charter and run by students, the Middleton Railway in Leeds. For one week in 1960 it ran passenger trains using a double-deck tram lashed to a diesel shunter, thereby just beating the Bluebell to the title of running the first preserved standard-gauge train. (The tramcar was later scrapped.)

The 'last train' on the Welshpool and Llanfair Railway under British Railways was a Stephenson Locomotive Society special on 3 November 1956. By then negotiations to preserve the line had started and by 1959 work on the ground to re-open it had begun.

Poster produced for the Festiniog Railway in 1965, when the green-and-cream livery of the coaches echoed that of Cambrian Railways and LNER 'Tourist' livery of the 1930s. From 1955 to 1983 the line was run by a former BR Eastern Region manager, Alan Garraway.

Above: Middleton Railway's Bagnall 2702 of 1943 and freight train passes under the M1 motorway in the 1970s. When motorway planners suggested they need not build a tunnel for such an insignificant line, Chairman Dr. Fred Youell asked if they could afford to man a level crossing 24 hours a day, as the line's right to exist dated to an Act of Parliament of 1758 – hence the tunnel!

Below: *Flying Scotsman* ready to depart on the re-creation of the non-stop run at Kings Cross, 1 May 1968. Filmed by the BBC, this run for many marked the passing of the steam age on Britain's railways.

There was by now a growing threat to the rail network as the rush for modernisation began to falter. In 1959 the Midland and Great Northern network closed to save a reported £20,000. Opposition to the closure led to a railway society that would eventually give birth to the North Norfolk Railway on a section of the M&GN. By the start of the 1960s Britain's railways had gone into deficit, steam was disappearing all over the country and the motorway building programme was well under way.

However, the dash for modernisation had also led to an 'official' approach to preserve some examples of Britain's railway past. In 1951, the year that the Talyllyn ran its first train, the British Transport Commission appointed its first Curator of Relics, John Scholes, previously head of the Castle Museum at York. Scholes quickly put together some roving displays and the search was on for premises for a Museum of British Transport (not exclusively rail). The museum opened in 1961 in Clapham, south London.

In 1958 a Consultative Panel for the Preservation of British Transport Relics was formed, prompted by the scrapping of some 'preserved' vehicles, this time at Stratford works. The membership included the SLS and other leading enthusiast bodies, including those representing tramway and road vehicle preservation. They faced an uphill task given that Robert Riddles, BR's first Chief Mechanical Engineer (once Stanier's chief assistant) felt it would be more practical to have carefully built models made of significant

Inside the Museum of British Transport, established by Curator John Scholes for the British Transport Commission in a redundant bus garage in 1966. Much of the collection formed the basis of the National Railway Museum, which opened in York in 1975.

machines rather than keep whole locomotives. John Scholes's appointment and the ad hoc arrangements for preservation by then happening across the network (plus the continuing presence of the former NER museum at York) undermined such a penny-pinching approach.

Despite the links between officialdom and the amateur groups interested in railway history, some machines didn't get listed for preservation, most notably Britain's first official 100mph locomotive – *Flying Scotsman*. In 1963 it seemed to some that railway enthusiasm had come of age when the rescuer of the Festiniog, Alan Pegler, bought it after an unsuccessful group rescue bid to 'Save our Scotsman'. Pegler's was the most prominent of a number of locomotive purchases, which had started when Bernard Latham of the Industrial Locomotive Society bought *Triassic* (a 2-foot gauge locomotive) to restore in his garden, closely followed by Captain Smith who preserved a Great Northern Railway tank engine (No. 1247) in 1959 with a lot of help from a sympathetic local BR management.

No. 1247 worked a number of rail tours in the early 1960s including one in 1962 for the Bluebell Railway with the incoming Chairman of British Rail, Dr Richard Beeching, on board. In 1963 his report, 'The Reshaping of British Railways' – described by the press at the time as 'political dynamite' – was published, and the writing was on the wall for railways throughout the country. Opposition to closures inspired by the report was widespread. From sit-ins on the track to filibustering over the small print, many people did not accept that closure was inevitable or even right. With the example of the

Built in 1895 for the Duke of Sutherland, *Dunrobin* once entertained royalty. Purchased in 1950 to form part of a museum on the RH&DR, it was sold to a Canadian businessman in 1964 and exported. In 2011 it joined a select group of railway vehicles repatriated to the UK that range from Southern Railway 'Schools class' *Repton* to a Darjeeling and Himalayan 'B' Class locomotive. *Dunrobin*'s new home is Beamish – the Living Museum of the North.

Jurassic at the Lincolnshire Coast Light Railway in 1967. The LCLR opened in August 1960 after some Welshpool and Llanfair volunteers based in Lincolnshire tired of driving to Wales (before the M62 was built). The LCLR existed near Cleethorpes until 1985 and re-opened on a new site at Skegness in 2009.

Bluebell Railway to the fore, they could also envisage lines run by the community for the community.

As the juggernaut of closure rolled around the country some of the opposition would lead to 'railway preservation' schemes, the original intention often being for these railways to remain a living part of the national network. The Keighley and Worth Valley Railway was the first of

LNER J70 No. 68222 from the Wisbech and Upwell Tramway in 1952. An engine and a coach from this railway were set aside for preservation after withdrawal but cut up in 1957. The outcry from knowledgeable enthusiasts led to the 'Consultative Panel for the Preservation of British Transport Relics', which co-ordinated seventeen societies and produced a list of what should be preserved.

this new wave of 'independent' community railways. Later the Mid-Hants Railway would start as the 'Winchester and Alton Preservation Scheme', the Great Central Railway as the 'Main Line Steam Trust', the West Somerset Railway as the 'Minehead Railway Preservation Society', and so on. Some schemes started and foundered – such as that at Westerham and one at Radstock on a surviving part of the late-lamented Somerset and Dorset Joint Railway.

By the time the reborn Talyllyn was twenty years old, Britain's railways had changed radically, with a whole generation of enthusiasts engaged in the practical business of preserving and running railways throughout Britain. Challenges that would have seemed ridiculous in the 1950s, such as the Festiniog's 'Deviation' project (see page 45), complete with spiral and tunnel, were well under way. The revolution started by Tom Rolt and his colleagues had spread throughout Britain with the history of industry and the recent past now in some areas being as much cherished as the crumbling castles that once formed tourist highlights. A seemingly boundless energy from preservationists once again led to dire warnings about the movement over-reaching itself, but this was not enough to put off the founders of schemes where only the track bed remained (not even the track itself), such as at Blunsdon, Toddington and Llangollen. With these new 'track bed' schemes (requiring re-installation of tracks, signals and rolling stock), railway preservation was clearly moving into a new era.

Ex-Higland Railway *Ben Alder* shunting at Georgemas Junction in April 1952. Withdrawn in 1953, it was planned to preserve the locomotive but after being stored in a variety of locations and following an abortive attempt to purchase it, in 1966 it was scrapped. Photographer Pat Garland was the first Treasurer of the Talyllyn Railway Preservation Society.

Above: No. 8 *Hurricane* built by Davey Paxman in 1927 (and carrying a whistle donated by Sir Nigel Gresley) steams along the Romney, Hythe and Dymchurch Railway during the making of the British Transport Films feature, *Romney Marsh*, in 1966.

Left: Early days on the North Yorkshire Moors Railway, when work concentrated on the Grosmont to Goathland section. Here an inspection trolley has just returned from the section to Pickering, which at that time was considered to be beyond the capability of the society. Pickering station itself was for a time threatened with demolition to make way for a car park.

CARRYING ON

WITHIN TWENTY YEARS of the Talyllyn Railway's first full season as a preserved railway, Britain's railway landscape had changed utterly. Schemes to run standard-gauge railways abandoned by the state went countrywide, and rapidly moved on from initial plans to focus on local transport need to being leisure attractions focused on the steam age. This was prompted by the other major change during this period, the end of steam on British Railways.

In 1952 British Railways had over 18,864 steam locomotives in service. By 1972 it had just three narrow-gauge steam locomotives on the Vale of Rheidol Railway (crewed by local staff more normally seen driving diesels), and a network that was almost a third smaller and steam-free.

The response from the preservation community to the disappearance of steam started slowly but grew as the 1960s progressed. When the former Bangor Shedmaster John Dunn organised an appeal to buy an LNWR Webb 'Coal Tank' in 1958, steam engines were still being built. Dunn was a good example of a figure that would become crucial as the preserved railway movement developed; a professional railwayman and an active railway enthusiast, he had earlier helped the fledgling Festiniog Railway. As the railways rapidly changed, the professional railway community, active and retired, often provided the bedrock on which new schemes were developed. In some cases they not only provided their time and effort free during their days off, but also brought help from the 'big' railway at crucial times, for example with track maintenance, driving skills, and locomotive maintenance and repair.

Around the time Coal tank No. 1054 was being rescued, Noel Draycott founded the Railway Preservation Society with the slogan 'Don't Let Steam Die'. This was an attempt to co-ordinate efforts across Britain and would eventually lead to the creation of the Buckinghamshire Railway Centre, the Chasewater Railway and the Scottish Railway Preservation Society. In different ways all three have a record of creating a great deal from very little and now have an enviable portfolio of locomotives and rolling stock.

Opposite/below: *Clun Castle* departs Kings Cross station on a rail tour in September 1967. The locomotive hauled the last official Western Region steam train, by which time it had acquired a celebrity status. It was bought by a group led by Patrick Whitehouse, and kept at Tyseley thereby becoming the founding locomotive of the Birmingham Railway Museum.

VALE OF RHEIDOL
NARROW GAUGE RAILWAY

BRITISH RAIL (M)
DEVILS BRIDGE   DAY
TO   RETURN
ABERYSTWYTH & BACK
Lein Fach Cwm Rheidol   (4303)

THE ONLY STEAM
ON BRITISH RAIL
Date.. 0 2. AUG 197
Valid as Advertised
Issued subject to the Regulations and
conditions in the Publications and
Notices of the British Railways Board

№ 0 2 0 0 5

You may retain this
ticket as a souvenir
Gellir Cadw y tocyn
hwn fel swfenir
BR 4533

After 1968 the
Vale of Rheidol
railway, which
ran summer-only
services, was 'the
only steam on
British Rail', as this
ticket from the
1970s proclaims.

In 1960 the Bluebell Railway opened the first standard-gauge 'preserved' former branch line. However, at this time 'preservation' primarily meant stopping something from being scrapped. The problem of storage after something had been 'rescued' was always an issue, given the size of rail vehicles. Four schoolboys founded the Great Western Society in 1961 to ensure the preservation of a GWR steam 'auto train' (push and pull with the locomotive in the middle). Their example set in motion the preservation of a whole collection of Great Western Railway equipment but it took until 1967 before this found a permanent home at the vacant steam shed at Didcot. The railway centre established there would eventually host a short replica branch line and a working re-creation of Brunel's broad-gauge railway.

Individuals buying locomotives in the 1960s often just looked for covered accommodation for their machine, still with a 'museum' mindset that imagined objects nicely displayed but static. When Scottish enthusiast Ian Fraser, a former LNER locomotive engineer (and an enthusiastic traction engine owner), bought 4-4-0 class D49 *Morayshire* in 1961 he donated it to the Royal Scottish Museum, and followed this by buying Ivatt 2MT 46464 and presenting it to the city of Dundee.

Dr Richard
Beeching in 1962,
looking from the
cab of the first
main-line
locomotive to
be privately
preserved, Great
Northern Railway
tank engine No.
1247. Beeching
saw railway
preservation as
having a place in
the life of Britain
but not as part
of the transport
business.

Groups of individuals thought of the preservation of the locomotive first, and where to store it and whether to run it came later. Those behind the preservation of LMS Pacific 6201, *Princess Elizabeth*, found accommodation was a potential sticking point in 1962 when they received a letter from BR stating:

Buckinghamshire Railway Centre in 2010 with Metropolitan 'E' class No.1 (of 1898), *Swanscombe* (of 1891) and a 1926 built Sentinel parallel-running for photographers. The centre started as a depot for the London Preservation Society in 1964 and has flourished since.

Engines can be sold for static preservation only provided the purchaser has suitable accommodation and facilities to maintain the vehicles in a manner which could not bring any disrepute to the British Transport Commission.

The instigator of the scheme to preserve 6201, dental surgeon Roger Bell, was lucky to get all 165 tons of locomotive accepted for storage on a private

British Rail's last steam operation – the Vale of Rheidol Railway pictured in May 1978 in full 'Rail Blue' corporate makeover. The line was privatised in 1989 and is now owned by a charitable trust .

The first train on the Bluebell Railway (7 August 1960) was 'topped and tailed' (i.e. had a locomotive at each end) by Wainwright 'P' No. 323 and 'Terrier' *Stepney*. In the first season 15,000 passengers were carried, proving that a standard-gauge 'preserved' railway was viable.

siding at Ashchurch in Gloucestershire, otherwise it might well have been scrapped. Sir Leonard Fairclough (builder of Britain's first motorway, the Preston bypass), who preserved a Lancashire and Yorkshire 0-6-0 freight locomotive of 1896 in 1960, had at least got a yard in which to put his engine.

Meanwhile, Butlin's had got in on the act in 1962, eventually buying eight locomotives to act as unusual attractions at their holiday camps. The locomotives included *Royal Scot* and *Duchess of Hamilton* (now part of the National Collection).

Purchased in 1963 and repainted into its original GWR livery, 'Small Prairie' 4555 was used for a time in ordinary service and is seen here on a BR freight train on Hatton bank in August 1964. 4555 was an essential part of a scheme by businessmen to run a tourist railway in Devon that would led to the Paignton and Dartmouth Steam Railway and the South Devon Railway.

In 1961 ex-LNER traffic apprentice and future Viscount Garnock bought ex-LNER K4 *The Great Marquess*. He restored it to LNER livery and based it at a Leeds shed until 1969, although it was banned from running after 1967. Alan Pegler used connections from his stint as Industry Representative on the BR Eastern Region board to get his own rail-connected shed and an operational agreement when he bought *Flying Scotsman* in 1963. (Pegler was sacked from BR by Dr Richard Beeching, who was unimpressed by this degree of steam enthusiasm.)

In Scotland John Cameron, once noted as 'Europe's largest sheep farmer', created the Lochty Private Railway in 1967 so that he could have the pleasure of running his newly purchased A4 *Union of South Africa* through his own land. William McAlpine of the famous construction firm created something similar, but on a smaller scale, at his house at Fawley from 1965.

The Talyllyn's first secretary, Patrick Whitehouse (who, like Fairclough, owned a building firm), purchased his first steam locomotive, ex-GWR 'Prairie' tank No. 4555 in 1963 and initially used the ex-GWR steam shed at Tyseley as convenient local storage. (There were even stories of Whitehouse driving his own locomotive home from work!) By 1968, when steam was finished and a growing portfolio of locomotives needed a home, Whitehouse was able to found the Standard Gauge Steam Trust and take over part of Tyseley shed as the Birmingham Railway Museum.

The opening train on the Keighley and Worth Valley Railway steams through Oakworth station in June 1968. In 1970 the station would become famous as the main location used in *The Railway Children* film directed by Lionel Jeffries.

Bishop Eric Treacey's camera captures Steamtown in 1974 when it was at its most cosmopolitan, hosting engines from Britain, France and Germany as well as *Flying Scotsman*, back from its American adventure.

The Bahamas Locomotive Society, formed to purchase an ex-LMS 'Jubilee' withdrawn in 1966, settled on a rail-connected shed at Dinting near Manchester (where most of the society came from) and built it up as a steam museum from 1969. The Society moved to Ingrow on the Keighley and Worth Valley Railway in 1990 after their lease expired at Dinting. The A4 Locomotive Society bought post-war steam record holder A4 *Sir Nigel Gresley* in 1966 and settled at the unlikely location of the Lambton Colliery Railway's 'Philadelphia works' for nearly ten years.

In the North West, Dr Peter Beet, a Morecambe GP, purchased locomotives and encouraged others to do so. Dr Beet was also involved with the planned takeover of the former Furness Railway branch line to Lakeside on Lake Windermere and negotiated the storage of engines at Carnforth Shed for the scheme. When on 13 August 1968 'Black Five' 44871 dropped its fire at the depot for the last time under BR – the end of BR steam on the main line except for steam cranes – Carnforth had already become an unofficial preserved steam depot. By 1969, 44871 was just one of the stars at the new visitor attraction known as 'Steamtown'.

The nearby Lakeside and Haverthwaite Railway opened on a truncated part of the Lakeside branch in 1973. Carnforth itself went on to be an essential part of the main-line steam movement through to today, although it closed as a visitor attraction in 1997.

The 1960s' relentless destruction of the steam fleet had by 1967 seen Noel Draycott's idea of co-ordinated preservation fragment into many separate preservation schemes. Nevertheless, an energetic former naval officer, Peter Manisty, on behalf of the Association of Railway Preservation Societies, was busy co-ordinating groups and individuals wishing to purchase locomotives and liaising with British Rail. His successes included getting rival schemes to pool their resources to purchase 60532 *Blue Peter*.

In 1968 Manisty co-ordinated a 'package deal' with BR which included David Shepherd's 9F freight locomotive No. 92203 (bought following the artist's first successful exhibition in New York) and his 'Standard 5' No. 75029; the Merchant Navy Preservation Society's *Clan Line*; the 'West Country' *Blackmore Vale* (purchased by Bulleid Locomotive Society, largely formed from the shed staff of Nine Elms) tank engine 41290; former

Heritage railways swiftly took advantage of film crews seeking railway locations. 5212 was one of the last steam locomotives in ordinary service but this did not prevent the newly re-opened Keighley and Worth Valley Railway using it once 'preserved' to make some extra money in 1968, in this case for a Solvite wallpaper paste commercial.

The ex-LMS 'Jubilee' Class *Bahamas* providing footplate rides outside Dinting shed in 1971 during the 'steam ban' on British Rail. Bought by the Bahamas Locomotive Society in 1967, the locomotive was one of the first back on the main line when BR relaxed the steam ban in 1972. Dinting Railway Museum closed in 1991 and the society re-located to Ingrow on the Keighley and Worth Valley Railway.

Southampton docks 'USA' tank engine No. 30064; LMS 'Jinty' tank engine No. 47383; NER J27 No. 65894; and a number of coaches. The total cost was £21,125 – a considerable bargain considering these were locomotives fresh out of service, and even in some cases fresh out of overhaul. A number of them would form the Longmoor Military Railway in Hampshire; this was an abortive scheme that lasted a little over a year after locals complained of the potential dangers to children of 'hissing, clanking, smoke-belching monsters'. (Ironically today part of the route is under the A3 Liphook bypass.)

By now senior British Rail management also had little time for steam nostalgia. A steam ban was imposed after the end-of-steam specials of August 1968, broken only by Pegler's legal agreement for rail tours by *Flying Scotsman* and a few moves of locomotives after dark (including 'Standard 5' No. 73050, the future *City of Peterborough*). In 1969 BR sacrificed the Waverley route from Carlisle to Edinburgh to political expediency, prompting a brief but ambitious preservation scheme headed by media personality Bob Symes. Meanwhile Pegler tired of battling BR bureaucracy and took *The Flying Scotsman* to America.

The effect of banning steam altogether from the network was useful for those schemes just starting out, such as the Severn Valley Railway and the North Yorkshire Moors Railway, as it meant that effort was concentrated on get things running. BR staff who hadn't agreed with the hasty demise of steam found many a way to help these fledgling schemes at a crucial time.

Meanwhile 1967 had seen a railway policy White Paper that proposed using a redundant locomotive shed at York for a National Railway Museum. The plan for a national museum to be based outside London led to a media debate with preservation pioneer Tom Rolt firmly in the 'York' camp.

York was much needed, since those locomotives officially 'preserved' were scattered in often less-than-suitable storage around the country. In 1968, the Manager of Bulmer's Cider, Peter Prior, offered to take on one of the largest of these preserved albatrosses, ex-GWR *King George V* No. 6000 and restore it to working order, as a sales tool. A '6000 Locomotive Society' was soon formed at the company's Hereford base, with locomotive driver's son and Bulmer's employee Bernard Staite working as the marketing man for the locomotive's supporting group. In 1971 Prior negotiated a 'Return to Steam Special' with No. 6000 to 'assess the technical difficulties inherent in running a steam train'. The success of this tour ended the 'steam ban'. For three decades after that Staite was at the heart of the steam rail tour movement. In 1975 he became Secretary of the Steam Locomotive Operators' Association (SLOA) helping to co-ordinate steam rail tours on BR; thanks to SLOA, steam was back for good.

In 1975 the National Railway Museum opened at York shortly after a grand celebration and huge gathering of steam locomotives at Shildon to mark 150 years since the opening of the Stockton and Darlington Railway.

The Lochty Private Railway in 1971 with John Cameron's A4 *Union of South Africa* on his private line deep in rural Fife.

ROLLING BACK BEECHING

D R RICHARD BEECHING gave his name to a policy direction in the 1960s that attempted to strip Britain back to a 'profitable core' of railway routes. He was not entirely successful: local political considerations, even marches on Downing Street, ensured that lines listed for closure survived up and down the country. Those that didn't often had a 'preservation' scheme suggested for them, in some cases getting a foothold on site, and by the mid-1960s *Railway Magazine* reported on a 'proliferation' of schemes.

The first railway to get started as an 'independent' after the pre-Beeching Bluebell Railway was the Keighley and Worth Valley in June 1968, after a six-year struggle. Initially the locomotives proudly wore a specially created livery and the line even bought a diesel for potential freight services. It ran early morning railcars as 'shoppers' specials' and still does. The K&WVR line was purchased in instalments over twenty-five years and claims the status of Britain's first 'privatised' railway; ironically its founding father was the arch-socialist MP Bob Cryer.

In the Midlands the Severn Valley Railway started out in 1965 to preserve part of the line to Bridgnorth, another pre-Beeching closure. With the line from there to Alveley Colliery available for £25,000, the society struggled but by 1968 had held their first 'steam up' and by May 1970 had got a Light Railway Order, the all-important 'official' licence to run trains over the first stretch to Hampton Loade. The same year saw the line to Kidderminster for sale at £74,000: most of the money was raised by selling shares in the scheme, which gave travel benefits to shareholders. This approach to fundraising was pioneered by the North Norfolk Railway and over the next twenty years would be used across the country, making the preservation scene essentially self-supporting during its main phase of expansion. Between 1972 and 1994 the Severn Valley Railway had four public share issues, raising a total of £2.5 million. However, the rocky economics of the 1970s meant share issues did not always provide the funds to match a railway's ambition.

In the case of those fighting to retain the Winchester to Alton line (which closed in 1973), plans for a mixed commuter and steam railway backed by

Opposite: Ivatt '2MT' 46443 departs Bridgnorth on the fledgling Severn Valley Railway during a steam gala on 14 April 1968. 'Day Membership' costing 3s 6d allowed passengers to ride the trains, with the 'official' re-opening coming in May 1970. Peering from the cab is the former BR Birmingham Division Chief Inspector Bill Gillett. 46443 is now a regular on driver experience courses on the SVR.

Volunteers on the Severn Valley Railway examine the engine compartment of ex-GWR railcar No.22 in 1967. Only the Bluebell railway has stayed 'steam only' until recent times, most societies accepting diesels from the start.

'Terrier' *Sutton* crosses the road at Rolvenden on the Kent and East Sussex Railway in 1973. Immediately after the line closed in 1961 a preservation scheme started, but opposition from the Department of Transport because of the line's numerous road crossings meant that the first stretch did not re-open until 1974. Only recently has a return to a main line connection at Robertsbridge become possible.

the local council had to be scaled back when a share issue failed in 1975. A successful (smaller) share issue later that year left the Mid-Hants Railway as a rump 3-mile route, neither at Winchester nor Alton. Passions ran very high as the railway later pushed on 'over the Alps' into Alton by borrowing the money.

If the last major Beeching report closure was the Waverley route from Carlisle to Edinburgh, in 1969, one other major closure which provoked a similar degree of incredulity and passionate objection was that of the Great Central Railway, once part of Sir Edward Watkin's vision of an international railway, and built to the continental loading gauge. In the 1960s it suffered a decline that became known as 'closure by stealth' and by 1969 was mostly closed. In the same year the Main Line Preservation Group was formed, in the midst of the steam ban, with the aim of acquiring 'a suitable length of main line for the operation of steam-hauled passenger trains at realistic speeds'. Recognising that most preserved lines being attempted were branch lines, the group wanted nothing more than their own preserved main line – Captain Howey's Romney Hythe and Dymchurch Railway but at full size. They focused on the Leicester to Nottingham part of the Great Central and leased offices at Loughborough (GC) station in 1970, opening to the public in 1972.

By now a threatened and recalcitrant BR was much harder to deal with, and in 1975 the new Great Central, having operated for two years, was faced with a 're-valuation' of the line's assets which threatened to stop the scheme

dead. In the event a single line from Loughborough to Rothley was purchased. It would be a thirty-year struggle before 'Britain's only preserved main line' would get to look like its claim, thanks in part to a generous single benefactor (as to a degree had been the case with the Talyllyn Railway years before).

The fate of many lines following 'The Reshaping of British Railways' report of 1963 ('The Beeching Report') was total abandonment. This is Belah signalbox on the Stainmore route, still standing (just about) in 2005 having been closed in 1964.

Elsewhere as 're-shaping' measures were rolled across the country, councils tried to protect something from the wholesale destruction of a hard-won infrastructure by at least buying the land from BR. In the beautiful Dee Valley of North Wales, initial talk was of the possibility of a 'monorail'; meanwhile the track bed was left to grow into a temperate jungle. Eventually a local railway society attempted the impossible, acquiring the lease of 'ten miles of ballast' from Llangollen to Corwen in 1975. The Llangollen Railway Society was tasked with laying at least a linear mile of track within five years to get a long-term lease. They succeeded, using (like the navvies of yesteryear) only hand tools, and second-hand track. Eventually they too would go for a share issue, the £480,000 raised in 1990 going in part to secure the project's future by paying off its accumulated debt in getting so far with so little.

Llangollen is perhaps the most picturesque of the 'track bed' schemes starting in the 1970s. Others include the Swanage Railway, which grew

Llangollen Railway volunteers on Berwyn viaduct laying out concrete sleepers ready for tracklaying using only hand tools in 1984. The location is the same as that of the 'Santa special' pictured on the next page, though only the wooden fence on the right gives it away.

39

from an unlikely late Beeching closure of 1972, the Gloucester and Warwickshire, once a major secondary route which closed in 1976 (the society's bold ambitions enabling it to use the letters GWR!), the Swindon and Cricklade, the Northampton and Lamport, and the Lincolnshire Wolds Railway. Once again railway magazines questioned the perils of proliferation; however, by the time these schemes had got started another factor was at play.

When British Railways started scrapping steam in the 1960s it initially used the tried-and-tested method of returning locomotives to major railway works and cutting them up there. Pretty soon this method could not process the numbers of locomotives being sent for scrap, so BR turned to private rail-connected scrap merchants.

Most locomotives were scrapped within days of arriving at these sites, but Woodham's Brothers in South Wales was by 1965 too busy cutting up wagons as wagonload freight started to disappear, and by 1968 their scrapyard at Barry had over 200 locomotives stored there in various states of disrepair. Very soon the game was on to buy them for nascent preservation schemes up and down the country.

While most schemes started with an ex-industrial tank engine, nearly all would end up with ex-BR locomotives derived from Barry. Without this injection of muscle it is doubtful that many could have succeeded in quite

Most steam railways run 'Santa specials' – an idea first tried on the Keighley and Worth Valley Railway over forty years ago. Railways can get up to a third of their yearly income from providing the service. Here a Santa special passes through Berwyn station in December 2008.

A general view of Barry Scrapyard taken in 1971 when there were over 200 locomotives waiting to be cut up. The vast majority would in fact be rescued for railway preservation.

the way that they did. They were helped by the fact that at Barry locomotives sold for their scrap value, meaning that many groups and individuals had a chance of raising the initial sum, with the repairs needed to steam them again being funded over a much longer period of time. In the end Dai Woodham, a businessman and not an enthusiast would say, 'because of Barry there's a steam centre or a railway in practically every corner of Britain', and he was right.

The recently restored 6960 *Raveningham Hall* pictured at a developing Bridgnorth shed on the Severn Valley railway, c. 1975. The locomotive was built in 1944 and is one of seven 'modified Halls' to be preserved. It was the twenty-sixth locomotive to be rescued from Barry Scrapyard.

A JOURNEY THROUGH HISTORY
ON THE
SETTLE·CARLISLE LINE

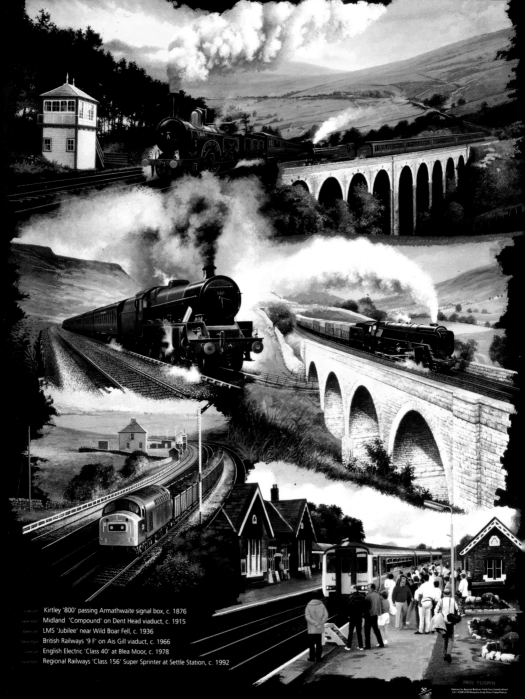

Kirtley '800' passing Armathwaite signal box, c. 1876
Midland 'Compound' on Dent Head viaduct, c. 1915
LMS 'Jubilee' near Wild Boar Fell, c. 1936
British Railways '9 F' on Ais Gill viaduct, c. 1966
English Electric 'Class 40' at Blea Moor, c. 1978
Regional Railways 'Class 156' Super Sprinter at Settle Station, c. 1992

PETE TURPIN

RETURN TO STEAM

IF THE 1970s had seen the instigation of railway preservation schemes across the country, with Beeching's late closures prompting more schemes and not-for-profit share issues funding most development, it was the 1980s when most of these schemes would reach a confident adolescence. The 'big' railway had by now overcome the trauma of Beeching's policies and was being run to the point where Inter-City made a profit and the costs of branch line support were clear.

Steam on the main line was co-ordinated by the Steam Locomotive Operators' Association over 'approved routes', with BR manager David Ward appointed to keep control of this part of the business. The new National Railway Museum under its first Chief Engineer John Bellwood was contributing by allowing some of its historic machines to steam again, including *Hardwicke* (built 1892), the 'Stirling Single' (built 1870) and the Midland Compound (built 1905). Bellwood, a good friend of preservation, had started his railway career as a 'premium apprentice' at Doncaster in 1944 and had been a volunteer driver on the Festiniog in the 1950s. He went on to volunteer for the Keighley and Worth Valley and was the North Yorkshire Moors Railway's Honorary General Manager and Chief Mechanical Engineer at the time of its official opening in 1973. Sadly Bellwood died of asbestosis in 1988 – a disease not uncommon amongst former railway workers, in an industry where the material had once been as commonplace as snow in winter. Meanwhile *Flying Scotsman* was also back from its United States adventure, 'rescued' courtesy of the unflappable millionaire enthusiast Bill McAlpine and its old manager George Hinchcliffe, who by now ran Steamtown at Carnforth.

Even the deep recession of the early Thatcher years could not dent the growing confidence of the railway preservation movement; if anything the 'quick wins' of privatisation helped. Changes like 'Tell Sid' (British Gas privatisation) put unexpected money in many people's pockets, and the job-creation schemes of the same period also got real work done that would have been beyond the reach of volunteers at the time, from scrub clearance to locomotive and carriage restoration.

Opposite:
Settle and Carlisle railway poster produced by the Friends of the Settle and Carlisle to promote travel on the route. The group was originally formed to fight closure proposals.

43

The 'Stirling Single' when operating on the North Yorkshire Moors Railway in 1985 during John Bellwood's reign as the National Railway Museum's Chief Engineer.

King George V departs from Paddington in 1985 during the Great Western Railway 150th anniversary celebrations. This was the last year the locomotive, famous for breaking through the British Rail 'steam ban' in 1971, was in steam.

Bill Parker, founder of the Flour Mill restoration centre in the Forest of Dean ignited his railway interest with the restoration (courtesy of a Manpower Services Commission job creation scheme) of a unique Great Eastern Railway 0-4-0 tank engine of 1876 for the new railway museum at North Woolwich. The latter was for a time London's only 'main-line' railway

museum (as opposed to the London Transport Museum) and was opened by the Queen Mother in 1984. In the long term North Woolwich Railway Museum was not to survive.

Meanwhile, even major changes like the demise of the metropolitan boroughs helped. When Greater Manchester Council disappeared in 1986 the East Lancashire Railway got a welcome cash boost, enabling it to swiftly leapfrog up the heritage railway charts by aiding its re-opening the following year.

Other triumphs came through in this decade. In the 1960s the Festiniog pioneers had been dismissed by the Central Electricity Generating Authority as 'merely playing trains' when they started a legal case for compensation because part of their line had been destroyed for the building of a power

Railway-related preservation in the guise of paddle steamer *Waverley* off Arran in 2004. Built for the LNER in 1946, this is the last ocean-going paddle steamer in the world and was preserved by the Paddle Steamer Preservation Trust in 1974.

Volunteers working on the Festiniog Railway's 'Deviation' project in the early 1970s at Archer's dam. The work to build this entirely new 4km line in the mountains of Snowdonia took from 1965 to 1978 and included a new 310-yard tunnel cut by Cornish tin miners.

Ex-LNER 'V2'
Green Arrow
crossing
Ribblehead Viaduct
on the Settle and
Carlisle Railway in
1988. Repairs to
this viaduct,
originally cited as a
reason for closure,
were completed in
1992 at a cost of
£3 million. Today
the line is in
24-hour operation,
and is particularly
heavily used for
freight trains.

station lake. By 1977 they had completed the Deviation – 2.5 miles of new line including a spiral and a 280-metre tunnel dug by Cornish tin miners. The first train back to Blaenau Festiniog (regarded by the FR as a 'restoration of services') was greeted with great festivities in 1982. The new Central station was supported by the local authority, here as elsewhere recognising the development potential that came from tourists spending money in the local area. Ten years after the Festiniog made it back to Blaenau, another early preservation scheme, the Welshpool and Llanfair, finally re-connected those two towns.

By now the idea of a 'working museum' had gone mainstream with Beamish, Ironbridge Gorge and Amberley Chalk Pits 'living museums' all getting into their stride and all featuring railways as part of the display. Beamish's railway included the re-located Rowley station and featured J21 No. 65033 of 1889 which had been kept from the scrap man by luck, storage and a series of moves by Beamish's founder Frank Atkinson. Rowley station's re-opening ceremony featured Sir John Betjeman, arch preservationist and TRPS member who through his campaign work was the saviour of great railway structures like St Pancras station.

Steam and tourism were by now well understood, but the idea of planning for future growth on the 'big railway' was still not embedded in government, and certainly not a government whose transport planning would eventually produce the white paper 'Roads to Prosperity' in 1989. So it was that the most popular route for main-line steam, the spectacular Settle and Carlisle Railway, found itself facing closure in 1983. The campaigners against closure had learnt all the tricks of the two decades since the Beeching axe and were eventually successful. Their case was much helped by Ron Cotton, an innovative BR manager who transformed use of the route – though he had originally been drafted in to help close it. Today the route is still a favourite for main-line steam, but also an essential freight route and open 24 hours.

The battle for the Settle and Carlisle Railway even saw the creation of its own 'Friends' organisation, a sort of public/private heritage hybrid that has helped restore stations on the line and encouraged the re-establishment of watering facilities for steam specials at Appleby and Garsdale, so far the only ones to be restored on a national network that once had these essential steam-age fittings everywhere.

The heritage railway movement was by now skilled not only in repairing and running railways, but also in lobbying parliament (both in the UK and in Europe) to ensure that its activities would not collapse under worthy but strangling red tape. Nevertheless, schemes like that at Radstock on the Somerset and Dorset failed (the organisation re-located to Washford on the West Somerset Railway); other casualties were to include schemes in Southport, Sheffield and Ashford. Meanwhile the British Isles' best-preserved narrow-gauge network, the 3-foot gauge Isle of Man railway suffered dark times with the lines to Ramsey and Peel dismantled and the historic inter-urban tram to Ramsey for a while cut back to Laxey. Douglas station, once a superb narrow-gauge 'Victoria' became a shadow of its former self before the island government saw sense and followed the rest of the UK in chasing the tourist market by nationalising the railway and investing in it.

35028 *Clan Line* was purchased from BR in 1967 by the Merchant Navy Locomotive Preservation Society. It is seen here in 1978 on the Settle and Carlisle line hauling a memorial train for the noted railway photographer and enthusiast Bishop Eric Treacy. The S&C was then an 'approved' steam route, at a time when 35028's home territory of the South of England had no such routes.

The big celebrations that had started with the Stockton and Darlington 150th parade in 1975 and followed on with 'Rocket 150' in the 1980s hit the buffers in 1985 with the announcement that Swindon works was to close. Celebrations to mark the GWR's 150th anniversary were bound to be muted after this body blow, which reduced a large engineering facility to a shopping mall. A rather good museum also emerged on the site, however, thanks to National Lottery funding. The Lottery was to prove a huge boost to railway preservation as its ample funds sought projects that made a difference throughout the country. Here it encountered extremely well-organised and motivated groups only too keen to apply for funds to develop and deliver their projects. Station restoration schemes, even locomotive rebuilds that once would have been a long grind, suddenly became possible as the largesse of a national gambling habit spread itself around.

Mallard steams out of York in 1987 after having been restored in preparation for the fiftieth anniversary of its world speed record for steam in 1988.

The NRM's flagship locomotive at the turn of the new millennium was *Green Arrow*, seen here on the Scarborough turntable in 2004. The turntable was re-installed with funding from the local council in 1984 and is a rare example of steam-age infrastructure being restored on the national railway network.

Engineering facilities keeping heritage railways moving were developed over time throughout the country, including at Tysley, Bury, Bridgnorth, Ropley, Crewe, the 'Flour Mill', Barrow Hill and Llangollen.

This period also saw the replacement of many BR 'modernisation plan' diesels, starting with the Western Region's diesel hydraulic fleet. In 1973 the Western Region 'Warship' *Greyhound* became the first main-line express diesel locomotive to be preserved. The 'Diesel Traction Group', which formed in 1977 out of the experience of preserving D821 and 'Hymek' D7029, proved that express diesel locomotives had widespread appeal – even if those running the Great Western museum at Didcot were initially

Four 'Deltics' posed at York, 5 November 1981. Left to right are 55015 *Tulyar*, 55022 *Royal Scots Grey*, 55009 *Alicydon* and 55002 *Kings Own Yorkshire Light Infantry*. All are now preserved.

On the occasion of the centenary of the line to Mallaig in 2001 a 'Plandampf' (regular trains run with steam on the national network) took place, mostly in appalling weather. In a rare break from the rain a returning train crosses Glenfinnan viaduct, now well known because of the huge success of the *Harry Potter* films.

unimpressed. When the Deltics ran their last train out of Kings Cross in 1982 it was said that more people turned out to watch them go by than had been the case with the '15 Guinea special' at the end of steam, and the event made the national TV news. Eventually five Deltics would be preserved and some of these would also return to the main line, as had (by now) many of the ex-Barry Scrapyard steam locomotives.

Even the impossible proved possible as the last main line express steam locomotive built for BR, *Duke of Gloucester*, was restored despite lacking its cylinders. The team responsible for this epic and complicated restoration even managed to put right the faults that had made the locomotive an indifferent performer when in service. In 1984 regular main-line steam returned, with the scenic West Highland line from Fort William to Mallaig ('the road to the Isles') getting a regular steam service in the summer months. Something similar had already happened on the York–Scarborough line, and would later on the Cambrian Coast line in Wales. Both the Mallaig and Cambrian lines would have closed had the Beeching plan been fully implemented. BR even for a time ran regular trains to the nuclear power

plant at Sellafield, which was going through a rebranding exercise; its former name, 'Windscale', had acquired a degree of negativity.

By the time John Major's government decided to privatise British Rail, the heritage railway movement was strong, established and confident. Inevitably a Minister was sent for a photo call to the Severn Valley Railway to drum up support for what private enterprise could do on Britain's railways. What SVR management told him about the importance of their huge volunteer corps to the success of the railway was of course ignored. Unlike pleasure railways, transport systems cannot run with volunteers, and even the good people who founded the Association of Community Rail Partnerships, building on the work of groups like the Friends of the Settle and Carlisle, were well aware of this.

Nonetheless BR disappeared in 1994 and for those photographing steam across the country a second golden age would eventually emerge as the whole railway became 'open access'. 'Approved routes for steam' became something of a bad memory and now charter trains could go almost anywhere hauled by steam.

Oliver Cromwell arrives at York Station on the Scarborough Spa Express in 2009. The locomotive was restored following an appeal in *Steam Railway* magazine in time for it to haul a re-creation of the '15 Guinea special' which marked the end of standard-gauge steam on British Railways forty years before, in August 1968.

BRAVE NEW WORLD

IN 2009 the TV motoring programme *Top Gear* featured a steam locomotive. So it was that all the grime and glory of a standard day's work for steam in the 1950s made it onto our screens in the twenty-first century. The locomotive was *Tornado*, the first newly built main-line steam locomotive to be seen in the UK since *Evening Star* was completed in 1960. *Tornado*, originally launched via a mass subscription scheme that aimed for 'a new locomotive for the price of a pint a week', was to be the most high-profile of a host of new build schemes. These aimed to fill in 'gaps' in the preservation record, as well as get over the issue that the main components on complex machines like steam engines were getting old. Those behind *Tornado* argued that with the youngest of the 'restored' engines now over fifty and the British main-line network getting faster and more congested, a new approach was needed if steam was to continue on the main line.

The £3 million *Tornado* grabbed the headlines across the UK in 2009 perhaps helped by the fact that *Flying Scotsman*, now finally a 'national collection' engine, was in the middle of a protracted overhaul. *Tornado*'s triumph was something that has previously only been achieved on the narrow gauge with the Festiniog Railway's new 'Double Fairlie' *Earl of Merioneth* (completed in 1979) leading the way. Twenty years later, the FR completed its fifth locomotive 'Single Fairlie' *Taliesin*; like *Tornado* this was based on a subscription method of fundraising where 250 people gave £10 a month for 12 years.

Successfully creating a new locomotive is no easy task, but this has not prevented others from attempting it. As with the FR, some of these schemes are about providing useful machines that will help heritage railways steam on through the twenty-first century. They include schemes to bring back to life extinct classes like the BR '3MT' and '2MT', the GER/LNER F5 and the 'Brighton Atlantic' *Beachy Head*. The latter is more typical of the new build schemes, as unlike *Tornado*, it started with an existing former Great Northern 'Atlantic' boiler and some other significant parts.

Similarly the Great Western Railway new builds, which include a 'Saint', a 'Grange' and a 'County', are all starting from a range of parts acquired from

Opposite:
Ex-S&DJR '7F' 53809 and 'Battle of Britain' Pacific *Manston*, both once residents of Barry scrapyard, re-create the authentic look of the 'Pines Express' on the North Yorkshire Moors Railway in October 2010. The 'Pines' ran over the Somerset and Dorset Railway until 1962. The S&D closed as part of the 'Beeching Axe' and today the use of the trackbed ranges from farm access and housing to a cycleway, two railway restoration schemes, and a narrow-gauge line.

other locomotives. The 'County' uses the modified frames from *Willington Hall* and a boiler from '8F' No. 48518, both of which were amongst the last ten locomotives to leave Dai Woodham's Barry Scrapyard in 1988.

Another project associated with the Great Western Society at Didcot is the re-creation of a 'steam railmotor', which was launched in 1998. The project uses an original 1908 'railmotor' (i.e. self-propelled) coach, with a new power unit built for it at Tyseley locomotive works and a new upright boiler built at Israel Newton's boiler works in Bradford. It has attracted Heritage Lottery Funding to the tune of £768,500 with final fit out and

King Edward I, once a resident of Barry Scrapyard, passes Rood Ashton Hall, also an ex-Barry engine, near Birmingham in 2002. This was the first time two ex-Great Western engines had passed each other on the main line for forty years and showed how far preservation had come in that time.

testing on the Llangollen Railway. Llangollen is also the main home of a project to build a new LMS 'Patriot' locomotive, *The Unknown Warrior*, which has the endorsement of the Royal British Legion and is intended to be quite literally a moving memorial to British service personnel killed in wars since the First World War. (The original Patriots were so called because they were intended as a memorial to the slain of the First World War when they first appeared in the 1920s.)

Meanwhile, Israel Newton has built new boilers for a number of standard-gauge 'Terrier' tank engines, proving that in the late-twentieth century, only for very large boilers like that of *Tornado* did you need to look abroad. (*Tornado*'s boiler was built at Meiningen works in Germany, Europe's largest surviving major railway works capable of steam locomotive work.)

Another twenty-first-century 'back to the future' move took place when Tyseley locomotive works re-streamlined *Duchess of Hamilton* in 2009 so that it looked as it had when new in 1938. This work was funded by the 229 Club, supporters of *Duchess* after it moved from the ownership of Butlin's (its original rescuer) to that of the National Railway Museum, and readers of

The Great Western Society's restoration of a 1908 GWR Steam 'Railmotor' from a derelict unpowered shell is the result of eighteen years of collaboration between engineers and societies, fundraising, and a substantial grant from the Heritage Lottery. It is seen here on trial on the Llangollen Railway in February 2011.

Steam Railway magazine. The latter had previously backed a number of 'return to steam' schemes including the original 100mph locomotive (if Edwardian train-timer Rous-Marten is to be believed) *City of Truro*.

Whilst some in the heritage railway world have been involved in headline-grabbing projects that look to provide the glamorous 'front end' on the main line, on heritage railways others have been quietly working on the 'succession' issue from the people's point of view. The Talyllyn has 'Talyllyn Tracksiders' – a scheme to get families with children involved from an early age. The scheme started in 1996 and evolved from a newsletter aimed at the children of Talyllyn members started by Christopher Awdry. Awdry's father had originally created the *Thomas the Tank Engine* stories to amuse Christopher when he was ill, and was an early supporter of the Talyllyn. Over on the Festiniog, 'Junior Weekends' were already in full swing, and the Bluebell Railway already had the 'Stepney Club' for children up to eight years old. These schemes have led the way in encouraging participation from a young age in the business of running a railway. Those who work hard to make them work hope that they will ensure a bedrock of volunteer support for the railways as the steam age becomes more distant.

Part of the same process has seen a number of railways build members' hostels to overcome the issue of where people stay when they come to volunteer at a railway, always a difficulty for lines remote from centres of population. The volunteers' hostel at Penrhyn station on the Festiniog opened as early as 1972, when volunteer accommodation on heritage lines, if it existed at all, meant sleeping in coaches. By building homes from home for volunteers, and encouraging young members, many railways hope to have cracked the problem of what happens after members of 'generation steam' are no longer around.

Calbourne on the Isle of Wight Steam Railway in 2010. Bought in 1967 by the Wight Locomotive Society, *Calbourne* formed the nucleus of what became a heritage line initially utilising 2 miles of railway purchased in 1971. Today the line runs to a junction with the electrified 'Island Line' that survived the closures of the 1960s. The IOWSR is notable for having no carriages in service built after 1924.

The advent of the Heritage Lottery Fund also meant that unglamorous but essential schemes could get funding, from carriage sheds to better facilities for disabled visitors. The Lottery also helped with some of preservation's recent surprises like the extraordinary re-creation of the country's oldest working locomotive 'Furness 20' of 1863. Having spent ninety years shunting in a steelworks as a tank engine followed by twenty years in a school playing field, today it proudly runs once again in as-built condition as a tender engine.

Railway societies even began to look at their own history; what had started as a few boards displayed at main stations aimed at recruiting new volunteers gradually turned into genuine museums, such as The Engine

In 2004 a short section of the Lynton and Barnstaple Railway on the fringes of Exmoor was re-opened. In 2010 *Lyd*, a replica of one of the line's original engines, built in the Festiniog railway's workshops and funded by a subscription scheme, visited the line.

The National Railway Museum's Class 101 diesel multiple unit at Ramsbottom Station, East Lancashire Railway in October 2005. When new these trains had been hugely successful in attracting passengers back to the railways. They lasted over forty years in service.

The first steam-hauled Royal Train for 35 years passes Llanfairfechan hauled by *Duchess of Sutherland* on June 11 2002. The crew included Gareth Jones, whose railway career started on the Talyllyn in 1951. The train later visited the West Somerset Railway, bringing a royal seal of approval to the heritage railway movement in Queen Elizabeth II's Jubilee year.

Opposite, top: Massed ranks of diesel gricers enjoying the Class 20 gala at Barrow Hill roundhouse in 2007. Barrow Hill is a good example of a preservation hybrid as it is not only home to preserved steam, diesel and electric locomotives but is also an operating and maintenance base for locomotives in everyday use on the railways.

House on the Severn Valley Railway, the William Marriott Museum on the North Norfolk Railway, and the Col. Stephens Museum on the Kent and East Sussex Railway. Often the museum building provided useful under-cover storage for rolling stock that was unlikely to be used again, and would otherwise have faded away on a hidden siding. It also meant that bequests of railway equipment had somewhere to go.

The closing years of the twentieth century saw a return to railway schemes that wanted to provide public transport links as well as providing steam trains for tourists. These public/private partnerships echoed the aspirations of the original standard-gauge preservationists. They were mostly developed from lines that had survived as freight routes long after the great cull of the 1960s. Passengers on the Dartmoor Railway at Okehampton could choose from a diesel service down the major part of the line or a steam train up a shorter section, with (once a week) a through train to the county town supported by the County Council. The Weardale line, in partnership with an American railroad company more used to working in the developing world, provided steam tourist services and a more 'workaday' train from Stanhope to Bishop Auckland. The Wensleydale line (beset by level crossings without automatic barriers making the whole line journey quite slow) attempted the same, whilst the Ecclesbourne Valley Railway on the Wirksworth line provided facilities for those wanting to do railway vehicle testing as well as train rides. The Mid-Norfolk Railway, based on a long branch line retained for grain traffic, helped with crew training for 'the big railway'. All became home for a growing fleet

of preserved diesel locomotives and diesel units, the latter getting their own co-ordinating group in 1998.

The Wensleydale Railway Society was formed after the saving of the Settle and Carlisle Railway had seemed to show a new dawn for railways in the UK. It raised £1.2 million in a share issue and was able to start passenger services in 2003 with the long-term aim of re-opening the whole route from Northallerton on the East Coast main line to Garsdale on the Settle and Carlisle. The Wensleydale line, like Dartmoor Railway, had been originally retained to ship stone from a quarry at Redmire. In the case of Wensleydale the army also had an interest as tank-loading facilities were available on the line, which is connected to the national network.

Below: Not yet two years old, 60163 *Tornado* is seen in charge of 'the Cathedrals Express' in November 2010. This Peppercorn 'A1' took nineteen years to build at a cost of over £3million. Prince Charles performed the official naming ceremony in 2009.

RAILWAY PRESERVATION IN BRITAIN

January 2011 and 'Hymek' D7017 (running as D7074) re-creates the last signalled train on the West Somerset Railway prior to closure by British Rail in 1971. Today the West Somerset is a flourishing heritage railway and D7017, purchased by the Diesel and Electric Preservation group in 1975, has been in preservation more than twice as long as it ran in service for British Rail.

Throughout their history heritage railways have fostered entrepreneurial partnerships and the new millennium was to see plenty of these. Diesel locomotives once discarded by the national network were re-hired in a variety of roles, and in 2007 a 'preserved' AC electric went 'main line' once again, later for a while going back into 'front line' service. From locomotive support groups to station adoptions and rail re-opening lobby groups like the Association of Community Rail Partnerships, members of these erstwhile 'heritage' schemes again and again proved the adage, 'if you want something done, ask a busy person'.

New builds, new ways of working and new members all mean that at the start of the twenty-first century heritage railways are embedded in British life

A train on the Welsh Highland Railway takes water at Rhyd Ddu. This scenic 25-mile line through the mountains of Snowdonia reopened fully in 2011 after over seventy years of closure and an epic rebuilding story. Both locomotives are Garratts built in Manchester for work in South Africa (the black one as recently as 1957).

55022 *Royal Scots Grey* had a twenty-one year career hauling expresses on the East Coast Main Line. Retired by BR in 1982 and purchased for preservation, many assumed it would never again run on the national network. It made it back onto the network in 1996 and today is one of a small number of preserved diesel locomotives in use on rail tours throughout the UK. 55022 is pictured running near York in July 2010.

to the point where they draw interest from other countries. Near neighbours France, Germany, Belgium and the Netherlands have something similar, but the sheer range, quality and attractiveness to tourism that Britain's preserved railway sector represents mean that foreign delegations studying their apparent success are not uncommon, a phenomenon helped by the offshoot of the Heritage Railway Association: Fedecrail – the European Federation of Museum and Tourist Railways, which was started in 1994.

Today, tourist railways with supporting volunteer groups are found worldwide. The age of heavy industry in the UK may be almost past, but its glories are celebrated, and the country that gave the world the railway has, appropriately, a richer heritage of railway activity than any other.

The first steam train from Swanage to London since 1966 departs Corfe Castle station on 2 May 2009. Closed by British Rail in 1972 and the track lifted, this scenic branch line was relaid by the Swanage Railway Society from 1977 onwards. In 2002 it was reconnected with the national network. The train is hauled by 34067 *Tangmere*, which from 1965 to 1981 was in Barry Scrapyard, and returned to steam in 2003.

PLACES TO VISIT

There are 108 operating Railways and 60 steam centres operating throughout the UK and Eire. For more information go to www.heritagerailways.com or contact the Heritage Railway Association, 2 Littlestone Road, New Romney, Kent, TN28 8PL. Below is a list of some of the railways in each area.

EAST ANGLIA

Nene Valley Railway, Wansford, Station, Stibbington, Peterborough PE8 6LR. Telephone: 01780 784444. Website: www.nvr.org.uk

North Norfolk Railway, Sheringham Station, Station Approach, Sheringham, Norfolk, NR26 8RA.
Telephone: 01263 820800. Website: www.nnrailway.co.uk

MIDLANDS

Didcot Railway Centre, Didcot, Oxfordshire, England OX11 7NJ. Telephone: 01235 817200. Website: www.didcotrailwaycentre.org.uk

Gloucestershire Warwickshire Railway, The Railway Station, Toddington, Gloucestershire GL54 5DT.
Telephone: 01242 621405. Website: www.gwsr.com

Midland Railway Centre, Butterley Station, Ripley, Derbyshire, DE5 3QZ. Telephone: 01773 747674. Website: www.midlandrailwaycentre.co.uk

Severn Valley Railway, The Railway Station, Bewdley, Worcestershire DY12 1BG. Telephone: 01299 403 816. Website: www.svr.co.uk

NORTH

East Lancashire Railway, Bolton Street Station, Bolton Street, Bury BL9 0EY. Telephone: 0161 764 7790. Website: www.eastlancsrailway.org.uk

Keighley and Worth Valley Railway, The Railway Station, Haworth, Keighley, West Yorkshire BD22 8NJ.
Telephone: 01535 645214. Website: www.kwvr.co.uk

North Yorkshire Moors Railway, 12 Park Street, Pickering, North Yorkshire YO18 7AJ. Telephone: 01751 472508. Website: www.nymr.co.uk

Middleton Railway, The Station, Moor Road, Hunslet, Leeds LS10 2JQ. Telephone: 0845 680 1785. Website: www.middletonrailway.org.uk

SOUTH

Bluebell Railway, Sheffield Park Station, East Sussex, TN22 3QL. Telephone: 01825 720800. Website: www.bluebell-railway.co.uk

Isle of Wight Steam Railway, The Railway Station, Havenstreet, Isle of Wight PO33 4DS. Telephone: 01983 882204. Website: www.iwsteamrailway.co.uk

Kent and East Sussex Railway, Tenterden Town Station, Station Rd, Tenterden, Kent. TN30 6HE.
Telepone: 01580 765 155. Website: www.kesr.org.uk

Mid-Hants Railway – Watercress Line, The Railway Station, Station Road, Alresford, Hampshire SO24 9JG.
Tel: 01962 733 810. Website: www.watercressline.co.uk

Swanage Railway, Station House, Railway Station Approach, Swanage, Dorset BH19 1HB.
Telephone: 01929 425 800. Website: www.swanagerailway.co.uk

SOUTH WEST

Paignton and Dartmouth Steam Railway, Queens Park Station, Torbay Rd, Paignton TQ4 6AF.
Telephone: 01803 555 872. Website: www.dartmouthrailriver.co.uk

South Devon Railway, The Station, Dart Bridge Rd, Buckfastleigh TQ11 0DZ.
Telephone: 01364 642338. Website: www.southdevonrailway.co.uk

West Somerset Railway, Minehead Station, Warren Rd, Minehead TA24 5BG.
Telephone: 01643 704 996. Website: www.west-somerset-railway.co.uk

WALES

Festiniog Railway, Harbour Station, Porthmadog, Gwynedd, LL49 9NF.
Telephone: 01766 516000. Website: www.festrail.co.uk

Gwili Steam Railway, Bronwydd Arms Station, Carmarthen, SA33 6HT.
Telephone: 01267 238213. Website: www.gwili-railway.co.uk

Llangollen Railway, The Station, Abbey Road, Llangollen, Denbighshire LL20 8SN.
Telephone: 44(0)1978 860979. Website: www.llangollen-railway.co.uk

Talyllyn Railway, Wharf Station, Neptune Road, Tywyn, Gwynedd LL36 9EY.
Telephone: 01654 710 472. Website: www.talyllyn.co.uk

Vale of Rheidol Railway, Park Avenue, Aberystwyth, Ceredigion SY23 1PG.
Telephone: 01970 625 819. Website: www.rheidolrailway.co.uk

Welshpool and Llanfair Railway, The Station, Llanfair Caereinion, Welshpool, Powys SY21 0SF.
Telephone: 01938 810441. Website: www.wllr.org.uk

SCOTLAND

Bo'ness & Kinneil Railway, The Scottish Railway Preservation Society, Bo'ness Station, Union Street, Bo'ness, West Lothian EH51 9AQ.
Telephone: 01506 822298. Website: www.srps.org.uk

Strathspey Railway, Aviemore Station, Dalfaber Road, Aviemore, Inverness-shire, PH22 1PY. Tel: 01479 810725. Website: www.strathspeyrailway.co.uk

INDEX